Paws to Reflect

for DOG LOVERS

60 Devotions
〜 **on** 〜
Trust & Love

Devon O'Day and Kim McLean

Abingdon Press | Nashville

To
William McLean Johnston,
Chief Dog-Chaser, Cat Whisperer, Pony Wrangler,
Fence Mender, Hay Pitcher, Farm Explorer,
and Environment Protector
at Big Sky Heaven Blue Farm.
Thank you for your love of God's creation.
You are the future . . . lead on!

PAWS TO REFLECT FOR DOG LOVERS

Compilation copyright © 2015 by Abingdon Press
Selections from PAWS TO REFLECT: 365 DEVOTIONS FOR THE ANIMAL
LOVER'S SOUL Copyright © 2012 by Abingdon Press
All rights reserved.

No part of this work may be reproduced or transmitted in any form or by any means, electronic or mechanical, including photocopying and recording, or by any information storage or retrieval system, except as may be expressly permitted by the 1976 Copyright Act or in writing from the publisher. Requests for permission can be addressed to Permissions, The United Methodist Publishing House, 2222 Rosa L. Parks Blvd., P.O. Box 280988, Nashville, TN, 37228-0988 or e-mailed to permissions@umpublishing.org.

ISBN 978-1-5018-1010-7

Unless noted otherwise scripture quotations in devotions attributed k.m. are taken from the New Revised Standard Version of the Bible, copyright 1989, Division of Christian Education of the National Council of the Churches of Christ in the United States of America. Used by permission. All rights reserved.

Unless noted otherwise scripture quotations in devotions attributed d.o. are taken from THE HOLY BIBLE, NEW INTERNATIONAL VERSION®, NIV® Copyright © 1973, 1978, 1984, 2011 by Biblica, Inc.™ Used by permission. All rights reserved worldwide.

Scripture quotations marked "NKJV™" are taken from the New King James Version®. Copyright © 1982 by Thomas Nelson, Inc. Used by permission. All rights reserved.

Scripture quotations marked KJV are taken from the Authorized (King James) Version. Rights in the Authorized Version in the United Kingdom are vested in the Crown. Reproduced by permission of the Crown's patentee, Cambridge University Press.

15 16 17 18 19 20 21 22 23—10 9 8 7 6 5 4 3 2 1
MANUFACTURED IN THE UNITED STATES OF AMERICA

Introduction

I am amazed at the many roles dogs have in both in our lives and in our society. They can be a best friend or a lifesaver to someone lost or trapped; a soft, cuddly therapist for the traumatized or a valued family member. The day a dog lover gets a new dog or puppy is one of our best days—the day we lose our dog is one of our worst.

We are tied to these remarkable creatures because they love us unconditionally and patiently—they think their "person" is the very BEST. This is a reflection of how God feels about us. God created dogs for us and gave them the extraordinary ability to win our hearts.

In this book, Devon and Kim write about their experiences and love of dogs, and the personal and spiritual lessons they've learned from them. I hope that you take a moment to pause and be inspired by these reflections of love and trust.

Lisa Lehr
Abingdon Press

Let Sleeping Dogs . . . DREAM!

Awake, awake, arm of the Lord,
clothe yourself with strength!
Awake, as in days gone by, as in generations of old.
—Isaiah 51:9

Some days, Daisy, our three-legged Dalmatian, is curled in sound sleep, when Henry, the miniature schnauzer, comes along to torment her with a curious sniff. Henry's curiosity and agitation can rouse Daisy from a dead sleep to a ferocious attack in zero to six seconds.

As humans, we have a metaphoric sleep as well, spending a lot of time in a comfortable "coast" in life's holding pattern. We fail to live up to our potential and forget to heed our calling. We need to be awakened to a fresh new life, without taking the heads off those around us, being jolted, as it were, out of our day-to-day rut. How to respond? How do we change and become fully aware and awake? We have to let go of the old habits and let ourselves forge a new path in obedience. When we empty ourselves of the world, we can be filled with God's light. We must let go of comfort—something that can be truly terrifying.

When you see a sleeping dog lash out, it's not usually out of a mean spirit. It's out of fear. We react just as ferociously as a sleeping dog sometimes because we are afraid to become new—afraid to become God's full potential for us.

On this first day of the year, let us wake up into a new day, where we have love all around us to encourage us. Let last night's nightmare fall away and become today's glorious dream. Be courageous in God's new world for you!—d.o.

Pink Slips and Chew Bones

*Grace and peace to you from God our Father
and the Lord Jesus Christ.*

—Philemon 1:3

I watched the golden retriever I had fostered for six months ride away with her new "mommy" as she stared at me through the back windshield of that little red Honda. She had come such a long way from the frightened abuse victim placed in my care. Her eyes never left me as the car left for the horizon. There was a chew bone in her mouth. Her tail was wagging. This dog knew she was going to a new home. Yet, somehow, she wanted to let me know she was grateful. She knew the dark place she'd come from and where she was now going, and I was just the spot in between.

Some things are not meant to be forever. They are just meant to get us there. Every friendship, every job, every place we live, is just a bridge to learning something we need in order to become who we are to be. People leave us because their part in our journey is finished. We never complete anything without having a lesson to be learned. Good-byes always leave us with a piece missing, don't they? Change is always difficult.

If you are saying good-bye to someone, something, or some place, reflect on what you have gained from the time you have spent. Let it be woven into the fabric of who you are becoming. Just remember, nothing is taken without being replaced by more of what you need. Just as I had been a temporary caregiver for that beautiful golden retriever, she now has a permanent place to curl up and call home. Say good-bye with grace and hello with hope, and leave with a lesson. Nothing leaves until it is time to let go. Accepting loss only comes with God's help and the wisdom of time.—d.o.

You Can't Judge a Cocker by Its Spaniel

*When they go with their flocks and herds to seek
the Lord, they will not find him;
he has withdrawn himself from them.*

—Hosea 5:6

Outward appearances can sometimes be very deceiving. As a shelter volunteer, I soon learned that the most evil-looking dogs were sometimes the biggest sweethearts. And then, there were the cocker spaniels. They had those beautiful brown eyes. Visions of *Lady and the Tramp* came to mind as I would reach to pet them.

With one unanticipated sharp growl, I would get bitten. I was not prepared to be bitten by an animal that was cute. This was a breed that had been animated in Disney movies, for goodness' sake! This misperception happened more than once. The adorable toy breeds would growl and snap with no provocation, while the pit bulls and Dobermans would roll around on the floor with me in play. This is by no means a criticism of any breed, just an observation that outward appearances and public opinion can be wrong.

In ancient times, some Israelites spoke highly of God, while worshiping pagan gods on the side. The Israelites were spiritually hedging their bets, so to speak. Well, it didn't work with God. And hedging bets didn't work with me either at the animal shelter. I stopped trusting those sweet, sad eyes until I knew for sure that the animal in front of me was trustworthy. And I was delighted to find cocker spaniels who were.

If we put our faith in gods that can't be trusted, we can get bitten. But we forget that and often put our faith in careers, money, or material possessions because they look at us with their beautiful brown eyes. Then, when we are least expecting it, they turn and bite us, leaving us wounded and with destroyed spirits. But we have God who loves us always and who knows our hearts.—d.o.

Jack Loves Veronique

Though we stumble, we shall not fall headlong,
for the Lord holds us by the hand.

—Psalm 37:24

Our dog Jack fell in love with Veronique the day we brought her home, and she adored him. A full-grown Pyrenees-collie can be as intimidating as a polar bear, with a bark that thunders across the valley, but he was gentle as a lamb with the new collie pup. She jumped and nipped and yapped at Jack playfully, and he would look up at us with a twinkle in his eye that seemed to say, "She's pesky, but she sure is cute!"

Overnight, it seemed Veronique was tall enough to reach the latch on the front door. One day, we were all at home when a neighbor called to say he had our collie; she had been hit by a car. We didn't even know she'd gotten out! He drove her to us, and we rushed her to the emergency vet. Her pelvic bone was broken, but it would mend without surgery.

Our neighbor felt bad. I felt bad. Jack felt bad. Our neighbor was a kind man who had seen Jack and Veronique running around, playing as though on a big adventure. They were having such a great time that he was going to let them play before he checked their collars for a number to call. Then a car rounded the bend just as Veronique shot out of the woods. Both neighbor and Jack froze with fright as they watched the inevitable collision.

Jack was beside himself for days, until at last he could see that Veronique was going to be all right. She could barely lift her head, but she managed to give Jack a lick on the nose so he wouldn't worry. Jack seemed sorry for not taking better care of his girl, for leading her to a dangerous place. And I learned, too, to keep the door locked even though Veronique no longer tries to dash past the threshold before I've given the okay.

We make mistakes. And sometimes our mistakes hurt the ones we love. But we don't have to keep making the same mistakes. God helps us when we stumble, and that's how we grow in grace!—k.m.

Divine Placement

Truly my soul finds rest in God;
my salvation comes from him.
Truly he is my rock and my salvation;
he is my fortress, I will never be shaken.
—Psalm 62:1-2

My dog Winston, a miniature schnauzer, used to wait on the left side of the sofa on his towel while I was at work. I would say good-bye and leave, and he'd hop to his place and wait until I returned. He'd be sitting right there in his spot when I opened the door. He'd perk up as I walked in, and when I gave the word, he'd run to me for hugs and kisses. Now maybe he wasn't there all day, but I have a mental picture of him waiting patiently and quietly until I returned to give him food, exercise, and love. He trusted that I would return, and he trusted that I would meet all his needs.

Even when other dogs entered our family, that spot on the sofa remained Winston's. Excitement, visitors, and hyper moments did not move Winston from his place. The other dogs could not get him to budge. I had given him a "place" and that's where he waited to hear from me.

I've had many dogs, but none ever understood the concept of "place" like Winston. He knew if he waited for my word, his rewards would be great. He accepted that waiting in his place was a good thing.

Patience to wait in our "place" given by God is not a common attribute. We are nudged from our place by peer pressure and people who want company in whatever they are doing. We get in a hurry to move or experience instant gratification, when real love is just about to walk through the door.

When we feel the fast-moving stomach-tightening anxiety urging us to be moving instead of waiting, let us just be still. Let us wait. The real voice we wait for is that of our Master. Waiting is not always easy, but when we are waiting on God, we will always find a blessing meant just for us.—d.o.

Good Dogs

See, he is puffed up; his desires are not upright—
but the righteous will live by his faith.

—Habakkuk 2:4 NIV

When one of our dogs gets a "that-a-boy" or a "good-girl," they prance around the yard, step a little higher, noses in the air. They have doggie pride. It's the pride of love and self-giving—a serving heart. That kind of pride reminds me of the scripture verse above from Habakkuk. When your dog fetches a Frisbee, or comes when you call, or does his business outside instead of on the carpet in the back bedroom, he is pleased to please you, as though he didn't even know he could be so good. He's been good, "upright," you might say, because you've guided him, not because he knew how to please you on his own. He would have been perfectly happy to poop on the carpet, until you taught him to do otherwise. He has faith in your guidance. He has faith in you because he loves you.

He doesn't know that he owes you. So, his righteousness is in being rightly related to his keeper—you.

We can learn from those "good dogs." On a profound level they can teach us something about a servant's heart, about pure motives and actions that are filled with gratitude. Love need not be mingled with self-centered pride. Real love is infused with faith. Your dog has a love-infused faith in you. And you, a love-infused faith in God. Our right relationship with God empowers us to love others with God's love, and all that right-relatedness is what righteousness is all about.

The miracle of God's love is made clear through the gift of Jesus. In love, he emptied himself in the ultimate sacrifice of self (Philippians 2:5-11).

Today, I will have faith in God to put pure, righteous love in my heart.—k.m.

One Voice

Listen to what the LORD says: "Stand up,
plead my case before the mountains;
let the hills hear what you have to say."
—Micah 6:1

The Great Pyrenees is a dog whose breed originated in the mountain regions of France as far back as 1800 b.c. They are often used to shepherd sheep. These dogs have a heavy double coat that enables them to be an effective deterrent to predators of sheep or goats.

Our family decided we needed a Pyrenees to help protect our farm from coyotes, so we located a rescue that had Great Pyrenees-collie mix puppies, where we picked out Jack, a little fluffy teddy bear. That small, cuddly stage lasted about a week. Pretty soon his feet were the size of feed buckets and his head was about the size of a garbage can lid. As we began to train him, we realized this big animal's feelings were easily hurt. He would literally become embarrassed at each correction, bury his big old head in his gigantic paws and cry. Some guard dog, we thought.

Then something happened. Instinct began to kick in, and this hairy beast began to run sentry around the outer edge of our farm. His baritone bellowing intimidated the coyotes, keeping them away from the farm.

Jack's bark was his greatest weapon against the coyote packs. When his voice echoed across the valley, he sounded eight feet tall. When Jack was healing from hot spots and had to wear a bell collar, he seemed thrilled with the effect of his voice, magnified to huge megaphone proportions. Jack literally sang across the valley, enjoying the power amplified by the huge plastic collar.

As children of God, sometimes we are called to sit quietly waiting for God's instruction. But other times we are called to boldness, to use our voice to stand up for what we believe in and to make our beliefs known. Then our voice, like Jack's with the coyotes, can be used for good.—d.o.

Daisy the Wonder Dog

I believe; help my unbelief!
—Mark 9:24b

I met Daisy the three-legged Dalmatian long after the trauma that caused her handicap and nearly cost her life. For the first time, when I heard her story, I realized how cruel people can be, how apathetic. I met her after someone ran over her and left her. It was also clear she had been abused. A tight chain had been around her neck for so long that it was embedded and infected. If my friend and cowriter Devon had not come along that road when she did, Daisy would have died. It was touch and go for many weeks. But she survived, and now she can run as fast on those three legs as the other dogs can. She's an amazing story. She's Daisy the Wonder Dog.

She's a bit edgy, as you can imagine. Her battle scars are not only physical. When we were first getting to know each other, she had to learn how to trust me. She was comfortable enough with me, but I quickly learned to be a little extra gentle with her so she wouldn't think I was going to hit her or punish her unfairly. Slowly she began to expect love rather than abuse from me.

She wants to believe in human kindness. When I pet her, she casts her big brown eyes up at me and makes the effort to wag her tail (which is not so easy when you are missing a hind leg), as if to say, "I believe in you, that you will be good to me. Help me even when I don't believe."

"I believe; help my unbelief." Those are the words spoken to Jesus in Mark's Gospel. Sometimes our faith and doubts live inside us at the same time, but if we love one another, faith will overcome in the end, with comfort, grace, and forgiveness. Daisy has helped my unbelief turn to faith, by her own growing faith in us.—k.m.

Grrrrrrr!

Seek good, not evil, that you may live.
Then the LORD God Almighty will be with you,
just as you say he is.

—Amos 5:14

Animals are like good-and-evil meters. Have you ever noticed that? Animals respond to innate goodness and innate evil.

I had a Great Dane named Sophie who was the biggest, goofiest dog in the world. She was a comedienne with feet the size of my hands. This dog got her head stuck in garbage pails, sat on a chair like a human with her legs crossed, and howled musically every time I sang. Sophie was just a big cuddle bug and loved everyone.

Then, one day we were out walking, and a maintenance man from our neighborhood association approached us. He always gave me a creepy feeling, as if he were watching me. My spirit kept warning me, but I ignored the feelings.

When the man got closer, Sophie pulled ahead of me and stood between him and me. Her hackles raised, a deep guttural growl began, and she turned into a wild woman! The man froze. I thought my "gentle giant" was going to have this man for lunch. A few weeks later, I was told he was arrested for breaking and entering some of the homes in the neighborhood.

People have built-in good-and-evil meters too. The Holy Spirit in us tells us about others, but also ourselves: where we belong or what places we should avoid, which might be harmful. He doesn't ever change those standards of the meter. He'll never order us to drop our integrity standards because business is business. He doesn't ever tell us to go into debt and not pay our bills to be closer to him. He does not ever tell us to be harsh to our children to make them better people. What he does tell us, that interior meter, is to seek good, always. And when we seek good, we find it.—d.o.

Fearless Faith

Do not fear, for I am with you,
do not be afraid, for I am your God;
I will strengthen you, I will help you,
I will uphold you with my victorious right hand.
—Isaiah 41:10

L ily is a sweet black dog who came to live with us when we agreed to board her big brother, Jack the horse. The two are inseparable, so we gave her the first stall on the right. We made her a cozy home with a doggie igloo and plenty of straw, which she prefers over the blanket.

Lily is old and wise. She can only hobble around because she has stiff joints, and her eyes are milky with cataracts, but she gets where she wants to go. She rarely comes up to the house with the other dogs.

One day, there was a severe weather warning, though the sky was perfectly sunny. With hardly a cloud in the sky, Lily came up to the house and found shelter in the hay bales we had stacked under the carport. She had not seen the weather channel, but she had gotten the message somehow that it was time to take cover.

An hour or so later, a strong wind arrived so suddenly and with such force that we barely made it to the basement. My son heard the thunderous roar first and yelled that we should take cover. Hail the size of golf balls began to slash the window screens. We were not in the basement for even sixty seconds and it was over. A tornado had twisted through, leaving a trail of damage. We immediately checked on the animals, and there was Lily, safe and dry, peeking out from the house of hay.

I thought of the Isaiah verse encouraging us not to fear, and realized that Lily had exemplified fearless faith in action. She must have heard that still, small voice guide her to a safe place, and God was surely with her. She was not even trembling after the storm, but looked quite calm and content. Today, listen closely for God's guiding voice in all of your circumstances. Lily's fearless faith is available to all of us, all the time.—k.m.

The Kindness of Strangers

For God will bring every deed into judgment,
including every hidden thing,
whether it is good or evil.

—Ecclesiastes 12:14

I have a friend, an executive with a deep love for animals, who, every day on his way to work, drove by a dog, noticing the creature and its environment. This particular dog was chained outside the owner's home with no dog house in sight. As the weather got hot, my friend started for work earlier each morning, giving himself enough time to leave a big bowl of water and food anonymously for the dog.

Each time, the dog looked up at him with a grateful glance as he drank the water as if he were in a desert and this a once-in-a-lifetime rain. This ritual was repeated daily, and the dog began to wait in happy anticipation for his new friend. Another anonymous present one night was a big dog house. Then he added a portable dog kennel with a cover. With every new gift, the time he spent with the dog created a bond.

So, one evening when he saw a car in the driveway, he stopped and knocked on the door. The owner of the dog turned out to be a nice person who had just taken on more than he was ready for with a dog. He wasn't mean. He was overworked and underpaid, and his circuits were just completely overloaded when it came to his life, and his dog's care was just a reflection of that overload. As he spoke with my friend, he began looking relieved at the prospect of his dog going to a new home.

Instead of instantly criticizing the young man for his poor care of the dog, my friend spoke of his own growing love and attachment to the animal. Change did not happen because of judgment but because of love, the only true motivation for good.

All the good works in the world don't pave our way into heaven. All our bad deeds don't keep us out. To God, every heart and motivation is transparent, and he compassionately deals with all he sees.—d.o.

The Beagle and the Cross

For the message of the cross is foolishness
to those who are perishing,
but to us who are being saved it is the power of God.
—1 Corinthians 1:18

Some things just don't make sense to the world. It's hard to understand in medical, black-and-white terms how holding a purring cat will lower your blood pressure. And it seems odd that rare hairless puppies in Mexico, when held against aching joints, can help reduce the pain and swelling of rheumatoid arthritis. The supernatural gifts between humans and animals have long been storied, but actual scientific causation and effect are hard to explain.

One morning while on the air with a radio show, I received a call from a distraught mother whose son had lost his beloved beagle. Her son was prone to seizures, and this dog was able to sense oncoming ones. The dog wasn't a trained seizure dog—he just had a gift he shared with the boy he loved.

Seeing an open door, the beagle had taken off in a chase of things unseen. The boy was inconsolable. An announcement on the radio led to the return of the boy's canine buddy, and all was well. And when the child called joyously to thank us for helping with the return of his dog, I heard such relief in his voice.

Important, life-altering realities can be difficult to explain. How do you explain the lifesaving power of the cross to someone who interprets its value only through intelligence? When you know how a life can be changed through the gift of Jesus Christ, it is impossible to keep that message to yourself. When we see someone struggling, even if they don't realize they are drowning, we still wish to throw them a lifeline.

The basis of Christ's love isn't primarily found in logic or empirical, verifiable data. It's found in testimony. Our testimonies are the lifelines we throw to those around us who are sinking.—d.o.

The Gift of Beauty

Esther . . . was fair and beautiful.
—Esther 2:7

Niki was our tricolored collie, born in North Carolina around the same time as my second child. Niki knew she was beautiful. She was unusual for a collie, like an exotic Lassie with her black coat, white mane, and sable accents. Her fur was long and sleek, her eyes expressive and wise. She was the perfect dog for small children because she was so gentle and patient.

Since summers in the South can get awfully hot for a long-haired breed, one year someone suggested that I get Niki shaved. I had never heard of shaving a Lassie-dog. They wouldn't look very collie-like, now would they? Hollywood might not renew her contract! Still, Niki wouldn't know the difference, and she would be so much more comfortable.

So I had her shaved. Boy, was she skinny under that thick coat! She looked like a greyhound with a really big nose. We laughed playfully at her, but she did not find it amusing. She seemed embarrassed. Niki was absolutely miserable for the rest of the summer. She was not herself, no longer outgoing and playful, no longer confident. I imagined this would be how a lion would feel if you shaved off its mane. She stayed inside during that summer, and I vowed never to shave her again.

One person commented that Niki was vain, but that wasn't true. She didn't have the sin of pride. Niki's story reminds me of the story of Esther in the Scriptures: Esther knew of her own astounding beauty and used it to save her people. Rachel, Ruth, Mary . . . all lovely, or so the stories go.

When someone is beautiful and does not know it, that's tragic. Every person I've met has a distinct beauty. Celebrate your beauty today. Cherish this gift. Celebrate who God made you to be.—k.m.

Just the Way You Are

Before I formed you in the womb I knew you.
—Jeremiah 1:5a

One day, I was reading the listing of animals up for rescue and adoption, and I found several "puppy mill accidents" looking for homes. Among them were the most adorable poodles, apricot in color, warm and fuzzy. Because of puppy mill inbreeding, they had been born without eyes.

Also on the list were tiny dogs born without front legs. These teacup Chihuahuas were adapting to little nubs to support the front of their bodies. Watching the videos of the little pups, I realized they were walking on their hind legs, learning to balance and deal with what they had. They weren't bothered at all by having what the world considers imperfect bodies.

Years ago, I read a story about a puppy in a shelter that was born with several abnormalities. The shelter was about to euthanize him, but the attendant, who had been fighting to save the little guy, felt something in his heart that said he'd be a perfect pet for someone. So he prayed for that perfect someone to come along. Later that day, a shy little boy came to the shelter. Suddenly he lit up! He spotted the puppy without front legs and made a beeline to him.

"Mom, he's just like me!" he exclaimed as he reached out to the dog, revealing arms that had no hands.

That puppy was God's gift created with a special boy in mind. He was perfect in all his imperfections, just as the little boy was. We have all been formed by God with unique callings, unique gifts. When we look in the mirror and see faults, God sees beauty. He made you to be exactly who you are. Every curve, every bulge, every bony knee, every gnarled inch of us is something that God calls beautiful and has a purpose for—God makes all things beautiful in his time.—d.o.

The Swimming Dachshund

The LORD . . . lays the beams of his upper chambers
on their waters.
He makes the clouds his chariot
and rides on the wings of the wind.
—Psalm 104:2-3

The world is full of beach people and mountain people, motoring road people and trail people. But one of the most fascinating groups I've encountered is lake people. Lake people have a culture all their own.

I accepted an invitation to join some lake people who weekly leave their condos to get on their houseboats and troll linked together across the lake to their favorite spot.

One of the boaters owned a dachshund, a dog bred for digging into holes and ridding farms of rats and moles. Dachshunds are not "lake people." However, this little wiener dog, with his short little legs and long body, wanted to join his canine buddies already enjoying a nice swim.

He barked in anticipation as his owners affixed a small, wiener-dog life jacket on him. He wasn't the diver the other dogs were, so the owners gave him lift-off, tossing him out into the water with his friends. His great big ears became wings as he took flight, looking more like a buoy than a dog. He hit the water and began churning those little legs with such joy, his fun-loving buddies chiming right in. One exuberant Labrador kept bringing him back to the boat in his mouth—I think the pint-sized hound enjoyed flying as much as he did swimming!

When we feel ill-equipped for life, God has ways of equipping us. When faced with a responsibility, we feel like we have legs like a dachshund when we need to swim. God can equip us for all our dreams. He wants us to fly! He wants us to swim! He wants us to splash around in our hope in him today.—d.o.

Stinky Smells and All

Thanks be to God for his indescribable gift!
—2 Corinthians 9:15

Love is a gift. Animals seem to know this better than people. Isn't it refreshing how uncomplicated pet love is? They either like you or they don't, and if they love you, you know it. When Josie, Jesse, and Veronique greet me at the end of the driveway every day when I come home, I think, "God must love us so much to have brought us together." They make me smile; I make their tails wag.

Love is not man-made. We don't manufacture it; God does. God loves every one of us, even when we feel unlovable. Paul wrote in Romans 5:8 that God proved his love for us by sending Christ to die for us while we were still sinners. Jesus said there's no greater love than to lay down your life for another. That's what love does. It gives all.

God's love is accessible. We can give love because God gives it to all of us. We have access by faith to the great love that created all the beauty around us. We have access through prayer to the peace of mind and soul that comes with knowing that the One who loves us most knows our every circumstance.

Love more than you need. Animal people do this so well, especially those who do animal rescue. They are gifted at knowing how to love the animals unselfishly. They make sacrifices of money and time, get scratched and kicked, and deal with stinky smells, all in the name of love; yet they don't think of it as sacrifice. It's a Jesus-attitude.

Wouldn't the world be a better place if we could look at people with all their quirks and peculiarities and find them as fascinating and worthy of love as we find the animals? Let's get in on the gift of loving today.—k.m.

Angry Little Dog, Big Loving God

There, above the cover between the two cherubim
that are over the ark of the covenant law, I will
meet with you and give you all my commands for
the Israelites.

—Exodus 25:22

My life had started out with such promise, and I was in the midst of plans to be a missionary. Then, without warning, several horrible things happened: a sexual assault, a loss of innocence, and the exercising of my right to choose as a result left me feeling abandoned by God. Bad things were not supposed to happen to good girls. I was nineteen years old at the time, and I believed that my promise had been stolen from me. I threw away my foundation and began storing anger deep within, hardening myself so that nothing could hurt me again. I was convinced that a God who let his precious child be so hurt was not the God for me.

So, God sent a little dog into my life. An aggressive little dog that no one wanted to be around was caged in the back of a shelter where I volunteered. His days were up, and he was about to be euthanized when something made me open his cage. His growls ceased and he jumped into my arms, licking my face, and letting me know that he was not all bad. I took him home that day, and he began to love me back into the belief that I was worth loving. When I stopped accepting God's love, God just sent love to me another way.

No matter who we are, we will eventually come in contact with pain. God is not in the pain, but he is in the healing. Forces whisper to us every day, saying that we are not worthy. The lies pick at our self-esteem and convince us that God is not there for us. But, God was. God is. And God will always be. That is our promise, and nothing, no one, can take it away from us!—d.o.

Odd Bedfellows

A friend loves at all times,
and a brother is born for a time of adversity.
—Proverbs 17:17

Our friends moved to a condominium, and with their children out of the house, there just wasn't room in their lives for the family dog, so we took him in. When the new dog arrived, we realized he was far into his senior years and had many ailments. He began to wander and get lost in the woods. He wandered so far one night that we didn't find him for two days, and when we did, he was too weak to walk back to the house.

Since he didn't integrate well with our other dogs or cats, we created a soft home of sawdust with an igloo and a nice dog bed in a horse stall. The Old Man seemed comforted by the boundaries, which must have resembled the privacy fence around the place where he grew up. He had a "runabout" each day, but only supervised ones.

We also had a wild, unsocial rescue cat named Squirt who kept her sour personality on full-tilt bad at all times.

One night, I was feeding the Old Man when Squirt strolled out of the igloo in his stall and began to eat with the Old Man. I was shocked. This unlikely pair appeared to be . . . friends! I later discovered that they cuddled up and slept together, this lonely old dog and the cat whose fear made enemies of all. Each brought the other comfort.

The last two years of the Old Man's life were not lonely because of an odd sweet friendship. Some of the best friendships can be born from life's hardest times, and even the hardest hearts soften when love takes root.—d.o.

Hi, Lily

You are precious in my sight,
and honored, and I love you.

—Isaiah 43:4

When Isaiah the prophet delivered these words to the children of Israel, he had already reminded them that God created them, redeemed them, called them by name, and delivered them. God wants his people to know that his love reaches beyond Israel's tribe to all people. God speaks this passage to people, but we make no mistake by taking it personally. One life makes a difference to the whole, while the rest of the family menagerie is precious to God too.

"Consider the sparrow," Jesus said. He was teaching us that to God, even a tiny bird is important.

When someone, person or animal, does not know they are special, it affects the way they perceive the world and the way they treat others. I guess that's why God made such a point of telling us we are special.

We have a sweet girl who came to live at the farm, a black dog named Lily, who did not, at first, know that she was precious to us. She is gentle and old, and her eyes are expressive and kind. Lily would not come up to the carport with the other dogs at dinner time, or seek the usual pats on the head. We thought perhaps she was not bonding with us, but in time we realized she wanted our kind attention as much as the other dogs did.

I often think about how people feel awkward, alone, or afraid sometimes, like Lily, and how others often misinterpret their actions as rude or ignore them completely. Some are less able than others to accept love. Trust must be earned. When I look to God's Word for understanding, I am reminded that the very best we can do is embrace God's very best for us, and then reflect his love with gentle patience. The more of us who know how loved we really are, the better we will be able to remind others that they are loved too.—k.m.

Footprints on the Pink Couch

Your path led through the sea, your way
through the mighty waters,
though your footprints were not seen.

—Psalm 77:19

The pink-and-white striped couch became the focal point of my new den as soon as it arrived—a perfect replica of a picture I had pulled from a decorating magazine and copied color by color. I had saved for every piece of furniture, each rug, and every framed print. Though I was renting, it felt like my first home. I stood back and surveyed the room, holding the picture up to make sure I had successfully duplicated all the elements of the professional decorators.

A gentle rain fell that night, washing the outside patio clean and turning the leaves a more vibrant green. I put a leash on my dog for a walk, and upon returning, he ran through the house with joyful abandon. Then, I saw the new pink and white sofa, a line of muddy footprints running up the seat cushions, over the back, and down again in schnauzer speed-racer style.

I rented a steam cleaner, unaware that steam would create a browning effect on the sofa fabric, so the tiny footprints became larger and larger ugly brown stains. No matter how I tried, the remnants of paw prints remained. Friends offered advice, such as "Get rid of that dog," but I decided that love for my puppy was much more important, invested in a washable slipcover, and enjoyed watching Winston curl up on the couch. The only one who knew about the footprints was me. My life was picture perfect again, and underneath it all, the unseen footprints represented faithful love to me.

God is like that for me. I can't explain tangibly how God shows, proves, and expresses his love to me every day, but I know that he is present. His path cannot be erased. When the world tries to wash away God's love for us, it just gets bigger. God's path is a good path, picture perfect . . . keep following.—d.o.

Dare to Trust

Jesus said to them, "Come and have breakfast."
Now none of the disciples dared to ask him,
"Who are you?" because they knew it was the Lord.

—John 21:12

My collie, Veronique, has very small eyes and a nose that catches every smell, making up for her lack of peripheral vision. People always ask me if she's blind. I tell them, "No, she just can't see." I've watched her befuddlement when we come home and pour out of the car as she tries to discern who is who.

I suppose that's how it was with the disciples when they encountered their risen Lord for the first time after the first Easter. They knew they weren't seeing a ghost. It really was Jesus, and beyond what their eyes could see, they trusted what their hearts knew.

I love how the gospel writer and disciple John writes that when they saw Jesus after his resurrection they didn't dare ask their Lord who he was. I'm sure Jesus would have understood. They could have asked, "Lord, is that you? Can it be?" But they didn't dare.

This was their chance to show the Lord, their savior and friend, that they finally got it. They had not recognized him at first out walking on the water, they had argued with him about the plan, the death he must suffer, they had slept through his agony in the garden of Gethsemane; but now, in this last chapter of John's book, they finally figure out that they can trust what their hearts know, even when they can hardly believe their own eyes. Perhaps they didn't dare question because they wanted the Lord to know they got it and that they were finally taking him at his word, and that's worth everything.

It makes me feel happy when Veronique recognizes me because I know she trusts that recognition of someone who loves her and will take care of her. She seems so relieved when I come home, like that means everything is going to be okay. And so it is.—k.m.

The Power of Prayer

*For I will restore health to you, and your wounds
I will heal, says the Lord.*

—Jeremiah 30:17

I have been in prayer with a group of sisters and brothers in Christ where someone has prayed for a sick or lost or wounded animal. These kinds of prayers often provoke snickers. I suppose it is only innocent concern that praying for an animal like one would pray for a person could be irreverent. Yet, our pets are family, they are precious to us. Many people love their pets with a heart full of joy and commitment and treasure them as gifts from God. So why wouldn't we pray for our pets? Would it be wrong for a farmer to pray that his crops will be healthy so he can make a living and care for his family?

I learned the importance of praying for our furry loved ones from my mother when I was a child. I had trained my collie, Shane, to avoid the danger of the road. Our driveway entered on the slope of a hill where cars tended to pick up speed and zoom by. My girl was always obedient, but one day, a car came out of nowhere and hit her. I was terrified and devastated. My Dad and I rushed her to the vet, and Mom went to her prayer place, knelt, and began to weep, asking for God's help for Shane.

As the vet examined her, I braced myself for the worst. She wasn't bleeding, but there might be internal injuries. She was a brave girl through it all. After lots of prayer and crying, I wanted to give the vet a big hug when he told me Shane would be okay.

After God healed my Shane, we lived on with gratitude and grace. He used my sweet dog to remind my family that he cares about the same things we care about. God wants his creation to be healthy, and he delights in our trust in him to heal us when we're not.—k.m.

Cheese, Please!

We speak God's wisdom, secret and hidden,
which God decreed before the ages for our glory.
—1 Corinthians 2:7

I sometimes pray that I will have the tenacity to search out the things of God with the same vigor our dogs have when they hear a rustle and go after it, or our cats when they catch a movement out of the corner of an eye and chase it down. We need to chase God down. In Genesis 32, Jacob actually wrestles with God's angel, demanding a blessing. Our little Jesse is like that. She, more than any of the other dogs, gets so excited about a piece of yellow cheese that she will jump, beg, sit, or dance the Charleston to get it. She won't give up. We shouldn't either.

God shows us a mystery, revealed in Christ. Jesus is the mystery, the door through which God's kingdom is unlocked and unleashed, the one through whom God has taken away the sins of the world. He is the living Word, through whom we become God's living message too (2 Corinthians 3:3). "These things," Paul says in 1 Corinthians 2:10, "God has revealed to us through the Spirit."

And Jesus tells us to search out that mystery: "Ask, and it will be given you; search, and you will find" (Matthew 7:7). Ask. Maybe faith is not about having all the answers; it's about asking the questions—not cynically, but with a true hunger to know. God welcomes our searching, without judgment. It's how we learn.

So what do we search for: what is our "cheese"? The Bible says our reward is God himself, whose precious presence brings peace to our souls. God's mystery answers your heart's cry now, yet unfolds more and more. Some days you might feel like you're the only one who gets it or as if you don't understand anything, but be like a schnauzer digging after a mole. Stay on it—the rewards will be great!—k.m.

Growling for Grace

A new heart I will give you, and a new spirit
I will put within you;
and I will remove from your body
the heart of stone and give you a heart of flesh.
—Ezekiel 36:26

Ever hear phrases like, "You can't teach an old dog new tricks"?

Well, you can! Our animals, young and old, learn lots of new tricks. There's another phrase often said about some people: "He will never change."

Wrong again! People change.

God wants to help us change for the better, and he does that by giving us a change of heart. He goes to great lengths in the Bible to tell us that he is patient with us if we're slow learners. People are not born with hearts of stone; there's a reason they harden. Sometimes they make poor choices, and sometimes they lack discipline.

As a result of these choices, people carry around blame or anger with themselves, which looks like harshness on the outside. Sometimes we simply don't know any better.

A heart of stone is a broken heart in disguise. On the outside, people see depression and anger, but on the inside there is hopelessness, despair, and fear.

We've rescued some furry babies who had broken hearts. They growled at us, snapped at the other dogs, and needed lots of TLC. They learned, though, and they responded to kindness.

Jesus heals broken hearts when we accept his love and grace. Trust him to soften you through and through.—k.m.

Bad Dog, No Biscuit

Therefore, since we have these promises,
dear friends, let us purify ourselves from everything
that contaminates body and spirit,
perfecting holiness out of reverence for God.
—2 Corinthians 7:1

My Great Dane puppy dragged me down the street; she ate a table as she began to get her adult teeth, and I found myself to be a lost ball in high weeds in regard to dog training. Dog treats were not enough to get her to heel, roll over, or even just sit. She was a big overgrown mass of muscle and did not understand my commands, whether soft or loud.

I called on a professional trainer to help me, and the first thing he did was take away all the dog treats. He said, "When you train them to work for a biscuit, you aren't training them at all. You teach them that the reason they are to do a behavior is for a reward."

His advice sounded like pure hooey. What dog would do what you needed him to do without a treat? But in her first lesson, my Dane was doing everything the trainer asked without a treat of any kind. She looked up at him adoringly and moved on the leash without so much as a tug. Her favorite reward was love, as it turned out.

We, as untrained puppies in God's world, might start out following God's rules and laws because we see some exciting reward in it for us. We seek to find favor or financial reward or even streets of gold when we die. We say yes! to Jesus because we want to avoid the fear-filled stories of a burning hell. But God wants us to love and follow him because we love him.

When the reward we seek is Jesus, then the desire of our heart will always be fulfilled, as he perfects us in a beautiful love relationship giving all of himself for all of us. Today, enjoy living and loving in the reward of simply . . . Jesus.—d.o.

Shades of Black

To him who is able to keep you from
stumbling and to present
you before his glorious presence without fault
and with great joy. . . .

—Jude 1:24

Black Dog Syndrome is a term that describes how the last dog to be adopted from a shelter is always a black one. All sorts of reasons are given for this phenomenon. The dogs from scary movies or who are used to frighten people are usually black. Hunters who breed for better retrieving dogs will have huge litters of black puppies and take them to shelters when they don't pass muster. So, shelters are full of black dogs that don't have homes, won't get homes, and will be euthanized by the thousands.

Sometimes the biggest crime that black dogs commit is being too ordinary. Since shelters get more black dogs than anything else, they simply don't stand out when people look for a new pet to adopt. They are part of a big crowd of sameness, so they are transparent or invisible. Winston Churchill even called his depression a "black dog."

Humanity has a way of judging everything. TV competitions, reality shows, and even ministry events with evaluation sheets can make us feel that we never measure up. We often fall into the transparent, ordinary category. We often feel like black dogs in a society that really prefers spots.

God judges so differently from the world. His judgment begins and ends with love and grace. Isn't it rich to know that God never ever sees a blob of alikeness in his creation? To him, we all stand out as his incredible handiwork, just like each big, beautiful black dog he made. One day, we will walk into eternity, and Jesus himself will present us before God, without fault and with great joy. That's what judgment looks like in God's presence. Today, live surrounded by love and the affirmation that we are never ordinary black dogs to God, even if the world says we are.—d.o.

Family of a Multitude

Then you, together with the Levites and the aliens who reside among you, shall celebrate with all the bounty that the Lord your God has given to you and to your house.

—Deuteronomy 26:11

There are lots of stray people in this world. People who have no family anymore, or who never did, or people who feel alienated from their families. Although sometimes, I think you hear more complaints from people who have families!

Our families are a blessing that disguises itself as a curse, it seems, or maybe we're just imperfect people often refusing to work together, robbing ourselves of the curious joy God intended families to be. Unreasonable expectations can get us in trouble. The son is expected to be like the dad or the daughter like the mother. But the truth is, people within the same family can be as different as night and day. We're all individually wrapped. You are not doomed to repeat the mistakes of your parents, and you are not a bad parent if your child loses his or her way. Life is bigger than that.

I think it might help us appreciate our own families if we learn from the attitude of our grateful strays. They know the value of a good family, flaws and all, as long as there is no abuse. We might get all caught up in how the house is never clean enough, but a person who has never had a cozy or friendly place to come home to won't even notice. They just soak up all the living that's been going on in your house. To them it's not messy—it's home sweet home.

If you are blessed to have a family, remember you really are blessed! More important, we all have a family in Christ. We're part of the family of God, and in his family there are no strays. Indeed, this family is eternal. We are privileged children of God, and with that privilege, we can invite others who are lost or lonely. If you need family around you today, rest assured there are people of God waiting with open arms to welcome you to a family celebration!
—k.m.

Who Let YOU In?

*"How is it that you, a Jew, ask a drink of me,
a woman of Samaria?"
(Jews do not share things in common
with Samaritans.)*

—John 4:9

I've often wondered why people jump to conclusions about a person's character so quickly, when they are so often wrong. We have a catalogue of templates in our heads, and we force everything to fit into one of them, making sweeping assumptions about people in the process.

I have noticed that some of our animals share this flaw with the human race. After all, the bird kingdom gave us the phrase "pecking order." Life in the wild is often survival of the fittest, and the fittest flock together. Bring a new horse into the field, and he will be bullied by the other horses until he has earned their respect. Add a new cat to the group, and she will refuse to associate with the others. Add a new dog to the pack, and things can get tense at dinnertime. But both human and animal can rise above these actions.

Veronique is our collie, and she is a most gracious hostess who rises above the natural instinct to insist that everyone get along. She tries to make sure no animal is shunned for being different. If a new dog growls at her, she whimpers sweetly and tries to get it to play. If a cat bats a paw at her, she nudges it with her nose and soon the cat is cuddled up next to her. She loves every new animal that comes to our farm.

I have seen churches that love the same way, where there is no judgment or assumption about race or sexual orientation and no raised eyebrows at someone who is divorced or at a young mother who has no husband. All are simply loved and accepted. All are welcome.

If dogs and cats and horses can all get along in the same family, why can't the human race? We're all part of the same kingdom, and God can give us the wisdom to know when to approach others with open arms. Today we may just have the opportunity to offer grace and acceptance to someone we've never even said hello to before.—k.m.

All We Like Sheep

There are different kinds of gifts,
but the same Spirit distributes them.

—1 Corinthians 12:4

Did you realize that there are two different types of sheepdogs? The first, the herding breeds, are extremely important because a scattered herd is a lost herd. The border collie is a breed especially adept at creating something called "bunching." They bark and nip at the sheep to keep them together in a bunch.

Outside danger from predators calls for a different kind of sheepdog. Where the herding shepherd is small and fast-moving, the pastoral shepherd is large and blends into the herd as one of them. Great Pyrenees pups are left with the herd to become imprinted. Herders work around the outside, but the pastoral dog works from within. The sheep bunch around the livestock guardian dog, pulling in close, protected by this unusually fierce member of their group.

Though these dogs can fight to the death against wolves and other predators, they usually use their booming voices to deter predators from coming near. The livestock guardian dog has unusually thick fur around the neck, so vital arteries are not left vulnerable. They have been given a flock to care for, and God gave them the exact features and skills needed to complete their job.

In churches, we have need for both herders and guardians. One person cannot fill all the needs of the people-herd any more than one type of dog can handle all the needs of a herd of sheep. You might be a herder by nature, or a guardian. God calls us to our place according to the gifts, talents, and personality with which we've been equipped. Now, you also might very well be the sheep, and the sheep must look to God, the Good Shepherd, for leadership and protection, always listening for his voice. But all are vital in God's kingdom, and God mindfully gives each person abilities to fit into his masterpiece.—d.o.

Love Is Bigger Than a Donkey's Ears

My brothers and sisters,
do you with your acts of favoritism
really believe in our glorious Lord Jesus Christ?

—James 2:1

Prejudice is a poisonous gas that seeps into the cracks and crevices of humanity, dividing as it goes. The racial discrimination that continued through the 1960s and 1970s, and even today with some people, is a dark example. The way women were and are often still treated on jobs and in marriages is another. Social classes look down on those less financially blessed, and people are labeled by a jacket or hairstyle.

The night two new donkeys came to live with us, the horses and dogs were beside themselves. The dogs looked to us for cues as to whether to chase these strange creatures off or round them up. The horses sniffed and snorted as Tucker pranced around with his tail in the air as though to show off for them. All were aware that these were not creatures we had 'round here before.

All were cautious, except, of course, the collie Veronique, whose first impression is always a loving assumption, but none seemed to say, "Donkeys? There goes the neighborhood!" Within the first week, the Tennessee walking horses and the donkeys were lying together in the field. The dogs calmed down and stopped chasing them, and the newest members of our family began approaching us affectionately. Those two turned our farm into a petting zoo, and even now their loud braying stirs up a joyous commotion.

The celebration of our differences has brought so much life to our farm. Why can't the people kingdom be a little more like the animal kingdom? Big ears, little ears; black, white; male, female; rich, poor—all things come together in Christ. Our job is only to love and accept. God can handle the rest.—k.m.

Sackcloth and Grace

Better a patient person than a warrior,
one with self-control than one who takes a city.
—Proverbs 16:32 NIV

Life is burlap. Its threads are coarse and rough, scratchy to the skin, so thick you could make a stencil of the crisscross pattern, and so sturdy you can use it to hold a sack of potatoes. A cat can lie on a burlap sack like it's as luxurious as silk. We, on the other hand, are not so fond of the rough places. When we make our beds on sackcloth, we always wish for satin.

Peace comes when, like our pets, we accept our circumstances with patience, knowing that someone greater than us has our best interests at heart. I always marvel at the way our dogs display that most difficult fruit of the spirit: self-control. They'll sit by a grill, jowls dripping, lips quivering, licking their chops, whimpering under their breath . . . and wait. Their restraint requires an extraordinary amount of trust. They obey because our love and respect are more important to them than a steak. Barely, maybe, but that counts!

Why is self-control so much harder for people? We consistently fall prey to our bad habits and desires. We smell the steak cooking and have to have it. We are unwilling to suffer the discomfort of longing. Overeating, charge cards, unhealthy but exciting relationships, or worry habits can be our big, juicy, medium-well, irresistible steaks, and we just want to leap on to the grill and seize our prize.

The dogs that have been lovingly trained are the ones that resist the steak. Like them, we can overcome many of the problems that wreck our lives if we allow God to help us or, should I say, train us. His word says in 1 Peter 1 that the trying of our faith teaches us patience. As we learn, we grow in grace, in patience, and in self-control. When we seek his help, moment by moment, God will fill us with his qualities, so that we can respond like God, no matter the temptation.—k.m.

"Bow Wow" Means "God Loves You"

Let your speech always be gracious,
seasoned with salt, so that you may know
how you ought to answer everyone.

—Colossians 4:6

Christians say certain phrases a lot: "The Lord is our strength." "All things work together for our good." "I'll be praying for you." Those ideas often sound strange or even trite to someone who has not been on the "inside." When Christians say these phrases without really thinking about their meaning or their effect on someone else, Christianity can seem like a clique full of people who presume to hear from God Almighty and have all the answers to your life. It's enough to send any sane person running the opposite direction.

I'm one of the Christians who uses those phrases, but I don't throw the words around lightly. We need to realize that the concept of God being "the Lord," and the Lord being "our strength" is not something everyone will connect with. Depending on the situation, religious language can be about as useless as telling your poodle, "The Lord is your strength!" while a German shepherd is chasing him. Better to pick Fluffy up into your safe arms than to recite ancient poetry at a time like that. Yet, that's what we do to people in need sometimes. They can be hurting or lonely, and all they get from God's people is an arbitrary, "The Lord be with you," when they really need someone to listen and understand.

Our pets don't take our words seriously until they can firmly associate them with kind actions. The same principle works when we offer words of hope to someone who is hurting. When we walk the walk instead of just talking the talk, acting as Jesus would, loving as he would, then God's glory is displayed in our lives. People can see firsthand that God is real, God is love, and God cares about them. Only then will our words bring comfort, filled with the strong reality of God in our lives.—k.m.

Magpie Funeral

My lyre is tuned to mourning,
and my pipe to the sound of wailing.

—Job 30:31

Marc Bekoff recounted in *The Emotional Lives of Animals* a scene about a group of magpies that had just lost a member of their flock.

Their comrade had been hit by a car and left lying on the side of the road. Each bird took a turn prodding to see if their friend was, in fact, gone. Then, one by one, they flew off and returned, laying grass over their lost friend.

In a photograph that circled the globe, Hawkeye, the canine pet of fallen Navy Seal Petty Officer Jon T. Tumilson, broke hearts as he lay prostrate in front of his friend's casket for the entire service.

Scientists have said that animals don't have emotions, that they just react to stimuli, but even the science world is becoming more and more aware of occurrences that can only be explained by emotional phenomenon.

We live in a world that pushes us to move on, focus on the positive, and keep our emotions in check. When did it become so important to get on with living so quickly that we can't feel anymore? We're not allowed to feel our loss, our hurt, and our pain as deeply or as long as we need, trained to think that grief is for the weak or imbalanced.

God hears the pain of the universe and never pushes us to move quickly through it to convenience him. God didn't chastise Job for mourning his lost children or tell him to buck up. In fact, God was and is consistently compassionate, urging us to bring our hurting spirits to him. In the demonstrative feeling of our pain, in the rituals of funerals, and in seeking God for comfort and solidity, God validates our needs, helping us find the peaceful passage to the next emotion.—d.o.

I will both lie down and sleep in peace;
for you alone, O LORD,
make me lie down in safety.

—Psalm 4:8

If you ever observe your pets all day, you'll notice a lifestyle that is balanced with rest and activity. Granted, they don't have bills to pay and are not responsible for gathering their own food and water, but they harmonize their activities. Our pets do not work themselves into a frenzy or sleep their lives away in a dark room. The cat sleeps, explores, sleeps, eats a little, sleeps, purrs, sleeps. Okay, so they sleep a lot, but their patterns have a rhythm and balance.

Ever feel like a slacker or been accused of getting old if you need a nap? Ever need to sleep in on a weekday when your job accommodates, only to wake feeling guilty? Ever need to go to bed early but choose not to after your friends tease you about missing the nighttime fun? Wouldn't it be nice to sleep when you need to?

Jesus did. He went to sleep in the middle of a storm, and he upset everyone's apple cart by doing it.

The key to a restful soul is a restful mind, so allow yourself to rest when your mind and body need it. Ironically, allowing yourself the proper rest enables you to be more efficient and get more done. We also need to allow ourselves our differences without judgment. Some people need less sleep than others. Some need a gracious plenty, and others are sleep grazers.

So, let the sleeping dogs lie and take a catnap because the Lord gives his children rest.—k.m.

Bark Nicely

But now you must get rid of all such things—
anger, wrath, malice,
slander, and abusive language from your mouth.

—Colossians 3:8

We have a friend whose dog can say, "I love you." She's been on television, in commercials, and circulated in video across the Internet. I think that if my dog was able to talk, "I love you" would be what I would want her to say. For a determined terrier to utter the syllables correctly takes great effort and lots of practice. An L or Y is a tricky business for the canine tongue.

Even so, I don't think I want my dog to be able to converse. Think about how often words get in the way of what we mean. Without a single word, my dog is one of the clearest communicators I know. With the wag of a tail or the move of an eyebrow, she can make me laugh or break my heart. I know if she's sad, happy, hungry, lonely, or concerned about someone. If I am sad, she will do silly things to cheer me up. She sits quietly with me on the porch when I write or play guitar. Words could ruin all that.

Words are a powerful gift and responsibility. We can use them as weapons—manipulating deals, arguing points, or cutting others down. Or we can soothe a hurting friend and inspire people to positive action.

We need to put the meaning back into our words, choose them carefully, and not waste so many. The Bible says our words should be "seasoned with salt," so that what we say is poignant and important, carrying authority to change people. Jesus promised the disciples the Holy Spirit would give them the words to say that would help deliver the good message of the gospel to people.

So start with something simple and pure to learn to speak words that are life-giving and healing. Our friend's dog has the right idea: let's tell God, others, and ourselves, "I love you."—k.m.

Cute as a Box of Puppies!

*For just as each of us has one body with
many members, and these members do not all
have the same function, so in Christ we,
though many, form one body, and each member
belongs to all the others.*

—Romans 12:4-5

W ell that's just cuter than a box of puppies," a lady at our church used to exclaim when she found something particularly adorable.

I love how a litter of puppies can all come from the same mom, but each is so unique. Even in a group of the same color pups, there will be definitive differences. Some will be fat, others aggressive, some sleepy, and some you just know will be a pack leader.

One night, my neighbor's hunting dog gave birth to a diverse litter. One of her little ones took to water immediately. One looked like the blue heeler down the road. Another was a fat black and red and white-spotted puppy that howled like a beagle. Every puppy was different and seemed to have been gifted with dissimilar abilities.

As they grew, their individual gifts all worked together to fill the needs on our neighbor's farm. The heeler rounded up the livestock, the beagle helped sniff out the rabbits, the Lab brought in the ducks during hunting season, and the big fluffy one kept predators away.

Even if you look at the people in your church or small group and think, This will never work, remember that God has placed us purposefully, with a job for each and every member of the body. When a room full of people from all walks of life can work together toward the same vision, maybe God sees a creation collection that makes him smile and exclaim, "Now, that's as cute as a box of puppies!"—d.o.

Where's Jelly?

You search out my path and my lying down,
and are acquainted with all my ways.

—Psalm 139:3

Jelly is a Pomeranian with a tricolor bouffant, and the personality to match.

Jelly likes to play hide-and-seek. We're always amazed how long that typically yippy girl can be quiet when she sets her mind to it. One day, we were pet-sitting Jelly and Phoebe (her sister). We were in charge of watching her, and then making sure she was safely locked in her cage before we left. When it was time for us to go, we told Phoebe good-bye with hugs and kisses, and then looked for Jelly to put her in her safe place. But she was gone. We called. But we didn't even hear a yap from her. Our hearts raced as we imagined all kinds of terrible things that could have happened and the sadness of this sweet family if they lost their little princess.

At last, out came Jelly, walking calmly out of her hiding place. It was a calm surrender, like she had thought it through and accepted that we were there to take care of her and that she should let us do that.

We also have our secret places, the corners of our hearts where we think God cannot find us. He searches for us and seeks us so we will experience his waterfall of love. God pursues us not in order to be punitive, but in order to help us. Those habits and dark places only damage our souls and our relationships with God, others, and ourselves. Sometimes we even place our health or well-being in jeopardy by the secrets we carry. But God wants to make us whole.

The good news of the gospel is there is nowhere too far or too hidden for God to find us. As long as you hide, God will seek you, reminding you of his love, that he created you, and that your life has purpose in his kingdom.—k.m.

Gray Stray Days

Jesus answered them, "This is the work of God,
that you believe in him whom he has sent."

—John 6:29

Sometimes when you rescue strays, you can just tell by their eyes and the way they cower that they have lost faith. They don't believe in people, nor do they trust any other animal.

Faith has a way of slipping away one day at a time as prayers seem to go unanswered, and life just gets harder. But God will give an animal discernment when the right person comes along that can help them. When life finally gets so bad that even pessimism seems positive, a sixth sense seems to kick in to let animals see through to the heart. After running from so many people, they suddenly know that you're the one who can help.

People have this gift too. It's the reason you know that a stray dog or cat is choosing you, or that you have to talk to a particular person. You can't really explain it. You're sent to help restore the faith of this animal, or you're the one who's despairing when you finally really see a friend who's stuck by you the whole time.

If you've ever had faith, you probably haven't lost it completely; it could just be very, very small. But the good news is that God never lets us go. Jesus said that faith as tiny as a mustard seed goes a long way in God's kingdom. So, with whatever you have, believe in God's promises, and he'll give you more faith. And if you've never had faith, God hasn't let you go, either; you just didn't notice he was there. Now that you see God, believe! Hold on to your faith, and on the days when it seems too hard, let God hold on to it for you.—k.m.

Abandonment Issues

For he has said, "I will never leave you or forsake you."
—Hebrews 13:5b

Whenever we come home from a trip, we can easily tell which of our animals have had hard times in their lives before us and which didn't. Veronique, the princess collie, greets us gently and goes back to whatever she was doing. She's glad we're home, but she knew we would be. She takes that for granted in the most wonderful way, as she should. Veronique's only had one home, never been lost, and never been abused or treated badly by anyone. She's been pampered.

Josie and Jesse, on the other hand, spent some time on the streets. They know the dangers out there, and they remember a hungry, hug-less life. So, when we get home, they jump on the car before we can even get out of it.

God can heal those old memories and hurt places inside us. He does it with gentle kindness, just like we do with our dogs. We let them come inside to feel reassured, and we give them extra hugs and attention until they understand that we're home to stay. They trust a little more each time we go through the process, but if they always need the extra TLC, that's okay. Love isn't so hard to give. Josie and Jesse need all the pampering they can get to help them remember what it's like for them now in the real world, the world at home on our farm.

As much as we want Josie and Jesse to know that we're never going to leave them, think of how much more God wants all of his children to trust his faithfulness and feel at home in his presence. He wants us each to know that we are precious to him, the apple of his eye. As we learn, time and again, that God is always there for us, trust grows, and so does our love for him.—k.m.

The Happy Hugger

Do not be afraid; you will not be put to shame.
Do not fear disgrace; you will not be humiliated.

—Isaiah 54:4a

Our friend Adam, an adult living with Down's syndrome, has a dog, Janie, who's always beside herself when thunderstorms crash. The thunder frightens her to the extreme. Adam understands Janie's fear, and when she starts whimpering, he puts his arms around her and holds her close until she is calm and the storm has passed. He doesn't scold Janie for being afraid. He doesn't explain to her that she has a roof over her head, so there is nothing to be afraid of. He doesn't tease her for being silly, about how she feels safer with her head under the bed. He holds her and comforts her and understands her fear is real.

Children and animals do not try to be truthful, they just are. I'm hungry. I'm sleepy. This hurts. They don't ask for

84

advice, reasons, or explanations for their needs. They just want comfort. Because they are children and animals, they probably are given comfort. This changes in adulthood, where pain, fear, and humiliation come with judgment, suggestions, and recommendations on how the problem can be overcome or managed, or how nothing is as bad as it seems.

We often miss what adults in need are actually asking of us when they are hurt or scared, trying to fix the problem rather than heal it. People, just like dogs that are scared of thunderstorms, need to be held and comforted until the storm passes. Comfort, rather than advice, can go a long way in helping someone you love through a hard time, and it never humiliates them or makes them feel ashamed of how they feel. We could learn so much from Adam in how to comfort during a problem, instead of trying to solve it, allowing God to heal simply through our hugs!—d.o.

Truth Serum

At the place where they stopped for the night
one of them opened his
sack to get feed for his donkey, and he saw his
silver in the mouth of his sack.

—Genesis 42:27

Helmut was the perfect inside dog. His owner claimed Helmut only had to go out three times a day. He didn't chew the furniture and came right home when he was called. You can imagine the surprise when a neighbor came knocking to accuse Helmut of killing his chickens. At that moment, Helmut rounded the side of the house, saw the two men, and did a quick 180, but not before his owner noticed white feathers hanging from the dog's beard.

Guilt is an awful thing. We carry it around our necks as if we can make up for what we've done just by feeling bad. When guilt hangs on, it is like a millstone keeping us from communion with God. Likewise, resentment is the millstone that people carry because of the guilty ones in our lives, and in the midst of feeling pretty superior, we commit sins just as grave.

The reading from Genesis comes in the middle of Joseph's story. He had good reason for resentment after his brothers sold him into slavery. Resentment could have been followed by revenge, but Joseph chose to wear forgiveness around his neck instead. When he saw his brothers, he had a feast prepared for them. He had been hurt beyond measure, by family members no less, yet he answered that hurt with love.

God does not say forgive when our enemies deserve forgiveness. We are told to forgive because resentment destroys our peace. The chicken was not coming back, no matter how guilty Helmut felt. But forgiveness from the neighbor and walking Helmut on a leash from then on resolved everything. Take the first step toward forgiveness today and see how, though it may not bring your metaphoric chicken back, it gives the new ones a better place to come home to roost!—d.o.

Is This Seat Taken?

So then, a sabbath rest still remains
for the people of God;
for those who enter God's rest also cease from
their labors as God did from his.

—Hebrews 4:9-10

Josie thinks she is a lap dog, even though she's big enough to jump up and put her paws on my shoulders. The funny thing is, she can actually crawl up into your lap before you even know she's done it. And she can pretty much make herself fit there too! If we are on the porch swing, she eases her way onto it. If I am sitting in a rocker, she slips up, one paw at a time, with the most subtle of movements. If we are by the bonfire, she wiggles her way to full snuggle position and looks up at you like she doesn't know how she got there. She loves her farm, her family, and her life so much. She's the happiest dog in the whole United States of America because she is loved and wanted, and she knows it.

I think God would be very pleased if his children knew just how much he loves them and were willing to relax in his presence and soak him up. Obedience would be not a question or a challenge, but a response. Less time would be wasted deciphering religious angst and misconceptions, and more time would be spent sharing the love that would overflow from within us.

Knowing we are loved is a foundational stone for the Christian life, and faith without this knowledge creates a harsh, condemning religion. God wants us to be like Josie and crawl up in his lap just because we like him so much and love the life he gives. That's what the Sabbath rest is about. It is holy confidence. It is obedience and faithfulness springing forth naturally out of a heart that is home in God's presence.—k.m.

The Hound of Heaven

Let us therefore approach the throne of grace
with boldness,
so that we may receive mercy and find grace
to help in time of need.
—Hebrews 4:16

Once you know Jesus, have had a revelation of who he is, and have committed your life to him, you can walk in that knowledge and grace. We don't have to rehash, rethink, and re-struggle. God always knows where we are.

One of my favorite movies is *Lassie Come Home*, which is about a collie that survives many dangers and meets interesting people, some bad and some good, as she travels an extraordinary distance. At last, because her heart longs for home, she finally finds her way back. The reunion is the happiest moment you'll ever see, for both child and dog. That's how it feels to find your way back to God and the confidence he gives us, but unlike Lassie, we don't always realize how much we were longing to be home with him. God knows, though—all along our darkened way, he knows, and he won't give up on us.

A poem, written in 1893, by Francis Thompson depicts the way God pursues those who run from him with his divine grace. The poem is called "The Hound of Heaven":

> I fled Him, down the nights and down the days;
> I fled Him down the arches of the years;
> I fled Him, down the labyrinthine ways
> Of my own mind; and in the midst of tears
> I hid from Him, and under running laughter.

I love that we can never be too messed up for God. Whether I've been the worst sinner or failed in my efforts to be squeaky clean, God always wants me back, and God wants you back too. God invites us to come near to him without fear because he's waiting to shower us with grace. Falling away doesn't happen overnight, but coming home can, because our loving Father is always waiting with open arms.—k.m.

Dog Catcher

Before very long, a wind of hurricane force,
called the Northeaster, swept down from the island.

—Acts 27:14

Animals are incredible indicators that something big is about to happen. Before a hurricane or a major storm, marine life will swim out to sea to avoid the waves that can throw them to land. Birds will fly inland seeking shelter. The barometric pressure will have even our indoor pets acting out of the ordinary.

But, unfortunately, people don't have the same warning system that animals have, and storms end up leaving stories in their aftermath. One story on the Louisiana coast began when a young woman felt so burdened to help with storm cleanup that she just loaded up her car and drove to the coast to distribute water and to clean debris.

On her first day, she noticed a dog barking behind a chain-link fence. She didn't pay much attention because dogs bark behind fences all the time. The next day, he was still there, barking. She took a closer look, but that was it. But when she saw him again on the third day, she stopped. Turns out, his owner had lost his life in the storm, and the dog had no one.

The young woman brought water and food, and after a few days, the dog came to her and allowed her to apply medicine. She brought the dog home, opening her home to the refugee.

God calls us to see what and who blends in to the background, especially when so many are hurting—the dogs behind fences, the faces in crowds, the broken hearts hiding behind a confident smile. We cannot remain comfortable bystanders in a hurting world; we must watch for the winds that sweep into people's lives, so we can be the first to offer God's love to them.—d.o.

Dr. Schweitzer

Be sure you know the condition of your flocks, give careful
attention to your herds.

—Proverbs 27:23

Hear our humble prayer, O God,
for our friends the animals,
especially for animals who are suffering;
for animals that are overworked,
underfed and cruelly treated;
for all wistful creatures in captivity
that beat their wings against bars;
for any that are hunted or lost or deserted
or frightened or hungry;
for all that must be put to death.
We entreat for them all Thy mercy and pity,
and for those who deal with them we ask a heart of
compassion and gentle hands and kindly words.
Make us, ourselves, to be true friends to animals,
and so to share the blessings of the merciful.

—attributed to Albert Schweitzer

A man can do only what he can do. But if he does that each day, he can sleep at night and do it again the next day," said Dr. Albert Schweitzer, whose commitment moved him to oversee the building of a hospital in Gabon, west central Africa, treating all living beings with respect, even those that caused problems. To him, even mosquitoes and snakes were not to be killed, but simply allowed to live and move on.

We often feel our chance to right wrongs is hopeless in the face of the sheer magnitude of need. There will always be another mouth to feed and another loss to burden those that choose to see. This simple prayer shows how Dr. Schweitzer took all of his one-man weakness and combined it with his all-powerful God to do what he could. He prayed and his daily life exemplified the commitment of his prayer.

He passed away September 4, 1965, and was buried on the banks of the river at Gabon, but his memory lives on in his hospital there. Because of his dedication to caring for those God placed in his care, many now share his passion. May we all live to inspire others by living out our prayers.—d.o.

You Don't Say!

Even fools who keep silent are considered wise;
when they close their lips, they are deemed intelligent.

—Proverbs 17:28

The old adage goes, "It's better to be silent and thought a fool than to open your mouth and remove all doubt." This phrase rings true whenever someone calls a particular smooth, gray-black dog a "hairless Chihuahua." No hairless Chihuahuas exist except for the poor souls with a skin condition. What they mean to call it, but probably can't, is a toy Xoloitzcuintli, so named after two Aztec gods. It's pronounced "show-low-eat-squeent-lee," and can be called Xolo for short. It is a separate breed, and according to the Xolo rescue site and the American Kennel Club, it was probably the first domesticated animal in the Americas.

Xolos are not the only dogs that are mistakenly called Chihuahuas. Another is the Chinese Crested. These dogs are believed to have evolved from African hairless dogs, but they sailed with Chinese mariners long ago. So, you see, you can't always judge a dog by its fur—or lack of fur.

The same goes for people. You can't judge a mother by the number of children she didn't give birth to (or did), or a man by the wife he doesn't have. A woman's worth is not in her husband, and a man's worth is not in his sons. Some people are specially called to be available to orphans and be friends to those who would otherwise have no one; and some people need to have some time to themselves, perhaps watching TV with the cat. Cats are brilliant conversationalists, you know.

When you see someone and begin to make a judgment call about who they are, remember first that, according to the Bible, Jesus didn't get married or have children. And several times he left his followers for a while to be alone and recharge. Instead of making an assumption about the people you're looking at, why not ask them about their story? Ask God to use you in their life or to use them in yours.—k.m.

Saint Francis's Vision

After this, the word of the LORD came to Abram
in a vision:
"Do not be afraid, Abram. I am your shield,
your very great reward."
—Genesis 15:1

The patron saint of animals is Saint Francis of Assisi, who gave up a life of wealth to serve God. Legend says he preached to the birds and prayed with a ferocious wolf who lay at his feet and never killed again. Many Blessing of the Animals Services use the following Prayer of Saint Francis:

Lord, make me an instrument of your peace.
Where there is hatred, let me sow love.
Where there is injury, pardon.
Where there is doubt, faith.
Where there is despair, hope.

Where there is darkness, light.
Where there is sadness, joy.
O Divine Master,
grant that I may not so much
seek to be consoled, as to console;
to be understood, as to understand;
to be loved, as to love.
For it is in giving that we receive.
It is in pardoning that we are pardoned,
and it is in dying that we are born to Eternal Life.

We can ask God for a vision for our life as we seek a deeper walk with him. Read about how filled with passion and love for God Saint Francis was. His dedication was answered—God showed him the special job he had prepared just for Saint Francis. Carefully listen to people and animals that come into your life. Give often, forgive much, and love always, and God will show you, too, the vision he has to fulfill your life.—d.o.

Stinky Dogs and Muddy Paws

Be perfect, therefore, as your heavenly Father is perfect.
—Matthew 5:48

When it rains, I sit on the front porch and write or play guitar. The dogs love it, running through the downpour to me, and reeking of wet-dog smell. I wouldn't dream of making them move just because I am overwhelmed with the aroma of wet farm fur. They don't know they're smelly, of course, so they expect the same hugs and affection. I've learned to wear clothing that goes nicely with muddy paws on rainy days. Even my car is marked by muddy cat paws that don't seem to wash off anymore. The car is their castle, the top of the world, and they seem so content there that I decided the car could just match my muddy-paws clothes.

Life gets dirty sometimes. Not unholy, not impure—just dirty. God's perfection is not cold, stainless steel; it washes into our messy world with grace. God lets us dance in the rain with delight. We can be drenched with the tears we cry, the art we make, the lessons we learn, and sometimes even our mistakes. Holiness isn't just about being clean. It's about wholeness, and God wants to touch our lives with healing, understanding, and guidance.

Sometimes we get the idea that holiness, as in squeaky-cleanness, is more important than love, but true holiness cannot exist without love. Love comes first. It's the first thing God told Israel in what is known as the Shema, the prayer repeated daily—love the Lord, and love others.

God says if we walk before him, we will be blameless, muddy paws and all. Blamelessness is a consequence of standing on holy ground, not a consequence of right action. The right action is born out of the holiness, as a loving response to a Loving Father. God's rules exist to protect love. People are like stinky, wet dogs sometimes. We need help sorting through all our messiness and being godly and clean, so God bathes us in his righteousness. All we have to do is get in the tub!—k.m.

Noses

And through us spreads in every place the
fragrance that comes from knowing him. For we
are the aroma of Christ to God among those who are
being saved and among those who are perishing;
to the one a fragrance from death to death, to the
other a fragrance from life to life.

—2 Corinthians 2:14b-16a

All dogs are descendants of the gray wolf, yet the domestic dog may be the most diverse species of all. If I didn't know better, I would never guess that the Great Dane and the toy poodle are related.

For example, consider the noses of dogs. My collie has a nose she could blow to Wisconsin, but my grand-dogs have petite Pomeranian noses. Pugs have nose inversions, while schnauzers have bearded schnozes.

But noses are not really about aesthetics; they're about smelling things. Some species know the power of smell for survival. No, that wasn't a black cat with a white stripe under the bush, it was a skunk!

People probably take the sense of smell somewhat for granted until something pungent wafts in the air, but we rely on it, too, for knowing when the food is good or when the house is on fire.

God likes things that smell good. Our definition of "good" and God's can be quite different, but Paul explains that those who love God emanate a sweet fragrance, a holy fragrance. Our prayers smell good: "Let my prayer be counted as incense before you," wrote the psalmist in Psalm 141:2.

The most poignant biblical nose analogy is the passage above from Corinthians. We are God's fragrance to the world. We smell like God from hanging out with him. And some people think we reek of God, while others think we're the best thing they've ever smelled. I guess we not only need eyes to see what the Lord reveals—we also need noses to smell.—k.m.

Do It, Jesus!

He performs wonders that cannot be fathomed,
miracles that cannot be counted.

—Job 5:9

A woman let her small dog out to take his morning break. When she heard insistent barking, she saw a grizzly with her dog hanging from his mouth like a salmon. Without a second thought, she ran out and punched the bear in the nose, and he promptly dropped the dog in her arms and ran off the other direction.

The dog had some minor bites, but was otherwise healthy. When asked about her actions, the young lady responded that she didn't think about her actions, she just acted to save her dog. We all are capable of doing seemingly stupid things in the name of love. At the source of every unbelievable rescue and every amazing miracle, God is our shield. We are always empowered by God to do the impossible, even when we don't realize it. I may not feel worthy of God working his incredible power through me, but God didn't put "worthiness" in the job description. God asks for one thing to be his miracle worker: a willing heart. That's all God needs.

When the day seems bleak and a problem seems hopeless, you get to put on the God cape. Cling to the promise that you can do all things through Christ who strengthens you, and you will be covered in a power so strong that all the forces of hell will shake in their boots.

Sometimes God sends a miracle, but it's not the one we wanted. People don't always live, and problems don't always disappear. Miracles happening all the time are defined by God and granted through God's big-picture lens. One day, we will see all of our miracle prayers in completion. Until then . . . keep asking, look for the miracles that you didn't have to ask for, and don't forget to wear the cape.—d.o.

You Are My Favorite . . . And So Are You!

Keep me as the apple of your eye;
hide me in the shadow of your wings.

—Psalm 17:8

I pick favorites. I can't help it! After hundreds of rescues, certain animals took bigger pieces of my heart. Finding Daisy the Dalmatian on the road and nursing her to health after she was hit by a vehicle ended up being a gift for me. She was sent to remind me that even when we've been left for dead by the world on a road out in the middle of nowhere, God sees us, hears us, and will help us.

All those animals that forgive our every mistake and still look up at us in adoration even when we feel like a screwup are God's reminder of his love. God knows that we don't always hear him when he tells us that we are forgiven and loved. When we won't receive his love, he might send a dog that licks us right in the face, so we can't help feeling loved.

As I look back, most of my favorites came along at the worst times of my life. When I was in an abusive relationship, God sent an abused dog that showed me how love could heal. When I lost my job, God sent me a miracle in my cat living through what should have been a fatal accident. God showed me that he could provide even in an impossible situation. When I felt fat and ugly, God sent me a golden retriever that looked at me as if I personally hung the moon. Yes, I have picked favorites but mostly when they picked me first.

God sent each and every one of them because he knew exactly what voice would reach me. He never gave up, because I'm his favorite. And what's incredible is that he gives the same, individual attention to every single person. So I'm his favorite, and so are you!—d.o.

Cleanliness Is Next to Impossible

Wash me thoroughly from my iniquity,
and cleanse me from my sin.

—Psalm 51:2

I had big plans for Veronique. From the start, I determined to develop clean habits with her. We'd be like those people you see on TV, where dog and owner are inseparable, and just like their dogs, her long collie coat would be silky and shiny all the time. She wouldn't have fleas or ticks, and I would be able to take her anywhere, because she would smell freshly bathed all the time. I assumed she would greatly appreciate this lifestyle, because she was from royal show-dog blood. Grooming was in her genes.

As it turned out, flaky dry skin from baths made her miserable. I tried doggy shampoo for sensitive skin, but to no avail. No problem, I thought, she'll just be an inside dog, then how dirty can she get? But she pined for the outdoors.

She whined; she ached for the green grass under her paws, the sunshine, and the freedom from the leash. So, I let her play outside for short periods of time. She decided at that point that "bath" meant "go roll in something nasty," which she always did. I finally gave up on the frequent bath plan, and you've never seen a happier dog.

Sometimes you just have to let a dog be who she is. I kept demanding that Veronique live up to my standards of cleanliness, when it wasn't her appearance that mattered. She is a happy, obedient dog, and does everything I ask her. She's got a clean heart, that's for sure.

Instead of scrubbing our skin raw, trying to make ourselves look clean to the world by never showing who we are, pretending that our lives are perfect, we need to reorient ourselves to God's definition of cleanliness. He's not fooled by our clean coats, but he'll take what's truly dirty in us and make it right. And the best part is that when God makes us clean, we discover exactly who he intended us to be.—k.m.

Lost Doggy in High Weeds

If you come across your enemy's ox or donkey
wandering off, be sure to return it.

—Exodus 23:4

I found Toby, an aged cocker spaniel, wandering in New York City. He had cataracts and worn teeth, but no collar. When I took him home, this dog spent several anxiety-filled months with me. One day, I had a friend walk the dog for me while I was working. She called me and said, "You'll never believe this. A woman just came out of the grocery store, took one look at Toby, called him Lancelot, and he went running to her! She says he is her lost dog!"

I was soon in the company of a young woman, originally from Kentucky, who had moved to the city. She had leashed her dog, which she had raised for thirteen years, to the park fence while she played Frisbee, so he would be safe to enjoy a nice autumn day. As she collected her things to leave an hour later, he was gone. I explained that I had found the dog with no collar and that all the shelters said that a dog of his age would be put down immediately, so I had kept him.

"I appreciate your loving him. I went to the park every day for six months and left food and water where we last saw him," she said.

That day, Lancelot's anxiety ended because he had finally gotten what he was looking for. He just wanted to be home, and now he was.

When we lose something we love, we must never give up hope that God has a plan in the works to help us find what we are looking for. When we find what someone else has lost, we might be a very important part of that same plan. Hope is one of God's greatest gifts. Whatever side of the parable you are on—the searcher, the lost, or the found—know that God wants everyone to find the way home.—d.o.

Choose a New Name

But now thus says the LORD, he who created you,
O Jacob, he who formed you, O Israel:
Do not fear, for I have redeemed you;
I have called you by name, you are mine.
—Isaiah 43:1

Sometimes when we rescue a pet, we don't know the pet's name. Its identity is lost, along with its past. The pet's story begins anew from that point on. Giving it a new name is an important aspect of its new life.

God deems names as important. He knows that all of us can feel stained and full of regret. We look in the mirror and see someone different than the person we wanted to be, and we can soon forget who we are, the person God created us to be. So God gives us a new name. With that name, he gives us back the identity that was stolen away in the wilderness and confusion. He redeems our life to make us clean and whole.

The passage in Isaiah 43:18 says, "Do not remember the former things, or consider the things of old." Habits that once prevailed begin to fade away as our desires change and line up with God's. The details of our life begin to come together, touched by his grace as he restores the broken parts.

In a moment's time, in the blink of an eye, he makes us new, though it can take us a while to catch the vision of what God sees because he sees the very best we can be.

The most special aspect of getting a new name is that God gives us his name, the name he chooses for us that identifies us with him. He says, "I have called you by name, you are mine." I love belonging to God.—k.m.

The Night Life

You are the Lord, you alone; you have made heaven,
the heaven of heavens,
with all their host, the earth and all that is on it,
the seas and all that is in them.
To all of them you give life,
and the host of heaven worships you.

—Nehemiah 9:6

A whole new world comes alive at night while most people are sleeping. Someone who is always on a morning schedule may miss the beauty of it altogether. I met a woman who discovered the nighttime magic of nature for the first time because of a less-than-magical reason: her dog was incontinent.

I met this lady at a United Methodist Church women's brunch. I finished singing, and she wanted to share her discovery with me. She said she'd been patiently cleaning up little accidents and dribbles she found in the house, but the hardest part was having to get up in the middle of the night. Her dog would quietly put a paw on her arm in the night when she "had to go," and I almost got the impression that the poor dog was embarrassed and hated to be such a bother.

As their new routine unfolded, the lady began to find the miracles in the quiet, mysterious wee hours of the morning. The stars were different, the air was softer, and one night, as she waited in the stillness, a magnificent owl flew over as though to offer a bit of wisdom: "Notice. Look around you. Isn't it amazing?" Her countenance was as bright as a child's as she talked about how she had never seen an owl before.

As she went on, I realized God had unveiled a world to her, almost like a waking dream. "I wouldn't have ever seen any of this if my dog had not been incontinent," she said. Her worry that she would have difficulty dealing with her new situation became a gift.

Blessings come in strange disguises.—k.m.

Strong Heart—True Heart

All kinds of animals, birds, reptiles and
sea creatures are being tamed
and have been tamed by mankind,
but no human being can tame the tongue.
It is a restless evil, full of deadly poison.

—James 3:7-8

In the 1954 work, *Kinship with All Life*, J. Allen Boone used his connection with an animal film star named Strongheart as a basis for his thoughts on the extrasensory communication between humans and animals.

The German shepherd was trained as a police dog, but was brought to Hollywood for silent movies. The dog worked in several films including the first version of *White Fang*. Although he has a star on the Hollywood Walk of Fame, most people remember his successor, Rin Tin Tin, better than they remember Strongheart. His breeding line is still going today.

In 1928, Strongheart's accomplishments were forgotten when he was accused of murdering a child. He was finally exonerated when the family admitted to fabricating the whole story. Truth won, but if it hadn't, Strongheart's life would have literally been over. Strongheart won over a nation, had books written about his communication skills and adept training, but even a wonderful dog like Strongheart would have been destroyed with a lie told by manipulative people.

Gossip is a cruel and dangerous evil. Repeated rumors are water-cooler weapons that are just as detrimental as straight lies, even if they never travel back to the subject.

We cannot un-ring the bell, so watching our tongues and our accounts of stories is our only choice as Christians. We have to guard our words as surely as we guard our souls, because Satan loves to tear us apart with lies. They occur one small deviation from the truth at a time.

We have to ask God to let the truth shine. Poisoned words almost shattered an animal that had no voice, but the truth shined through. Are we not just as protected by the truth?—d.o.

Grateful . . . Except for Broccoli

Let the message of Christ dwell among you richly
as you teach and admonish
one another with all wisdom through psalms,
hymns, and songs from the Spirit,
singing to God with gratitude in your hearts.
—Colossians 3:16

Yogi was one of the most perfect dogs God ever created. He was a beautiful, red golden retriever with a compassionate spirit and a sweet countenance that always made you feel better on a stormy day.

Holidays were always special for Yogi because the house smelled like cooking, and the leftovers were fantastic! Yogi would wait for his goodies patiently, and the only indication of his excitement was a single drip of saliva falling slowly toward the floor.

Yogi loved gravy over kibble, and he always seemed grateful for every bite! On one particular night, I added the leftover broccoli, thinking this would really make his tail wag, but when I turned, expecting to see empty, shining bowls, next to Yogi was an orderly pile of green broccoli stalks, sucked clean of gravy. Like a youngster who doesn't like his veggies, Yogi had spit out the part of the gift he didn't want in one big, "Yuck!"

God often gives us gifts that include a side effect of "yuck." Many times, with his glorious "gravy" comes the broccoli of life. We are blessed with a wonderful new job that demands more energy than we've given before. We are blessed with children, who eventually leave us with heartbreaking empty nest syndrome. With every blessing comes challenge.

What do we do when our favorite joy is laced with bits of broccoli? We thank God for the broccoli. God invites us to enter the greener pastures, and sometimes the green turns out to be broccoli. We have a choice to spit it out, or we can learn to honestly thank God that he cares so much for us that he gives us nourishing broccoli.—d.o.

Forgive and Remember

A person's wisdom yields patience;
it is to one's glory to overlook an offense.
—Proverbs 19:11

My first Christmas with Sophie, my Great Dane, was an adventure. In her heart, she was a small puppy, filled with mischief, but in reality she was huge in size and with teeth that could destroy an ottoman in a single afternoon. She was a force to be reckoned with that year around the Christmas tree.

Upon waking in the morning, I found a red wooden cowboy boot with its toe bitten off on her bed. She had stolen the ornament from one of the lower branches in the night and chewed until half was missing. One pointed look at her, and she hid the destroyed ornament under her big, blocky head, ears back and tail down.

I couldn't bring myself to fuss at her because she seemed to realize that she had made a mistake. I also could never bring myself to throw away the marred remains of the ornament. Each year it gets a special display, and we tell the story about the fate of the missing part of the ornament.

To this day, that ornament is a precious reminder to me of how God sees the mistakes we bring to him. Even when we disobey, going against his law of love, God's forgiveness is great and beautiful. He looks at the broken ornaments in our lives and hangs them, forgiven and precious, on the tree of life as a testament to his love for us. Our mistakes are not reminders to God of our failures. God forgives us fully and wants to display his glory in us. Our forgiven mistakes represent our true success in God's eyes.

We are the ornaments on the branches of God's Christmas tree, shining in beauty for all the world to see. Forgiveness is the gift that brings us to God's original brilliance, and our honesty about our problems and his forgiveness makes that brilliance shine from our lives into a world that desperately needs light.—d.o.

Disney Dog

I thank my God every time I remember you.
—Philippians 1:3

Tiffany Abigail was a Christmas present to my two daughters. I stuck a little bow on her head, and she completed the picture with licks and doggie smiles. We called her Abby. She was a beautiful blue merle sheltie with multicolored eyes to match her coat. I gave her to them early, just before December, because I knew it would be a sadder-than-usual Christmas. It would be the first one with just us girls.

I was worried about money, but I managed to save enough to take us, including Abby, to Disney World. So that year, we had a Charlie Brown Christmas tree because there was not a penny left for a bigger one.

At Disney, we found the most wonderful kennel, and though Abby was not thrilled that we were leaving her there, she was clean and safe. We came back to give her hugs just about every hour, and at lunch time we took her out of the kennel and had a picnic with her. No matter how fun each ride was, my six-year-old constantly reminded us, "We have to check on Abby again after this ride, okay, Mommy?"

It's funny to think about it now, but the thing that makes that year stand out from all the rest to me wasn't the sadness or bitterness of our situation; I remember that Abby was there. She made us laugh, and now that Christmas is a precious memory we share.

Our pets are an important part of our lives. They can give us comforting reminders in the midst of family tension or when the sad memories come. They bring us laughter and smiles as they join in on the celebration and festivity of the season. We miss Abby, but every Christmas, I thank God for her because she was the best Christmas present our family ever got.—k.m.

Heroes

He saved us, not because of righteous things
we had done, but because of his mercy.
He saved us through the washing of rebirth and
renewal by the Holy Spirit.

—Titus 3:5

I was asleep one night in a house I shared with two roommates, one down the hall from me, and one downstairs. Bill, our downstairs renter, had blown out a candle on the fireplace mantle and gone to bed after us. He didn't realize a small spark from the wick had blown to a dried flower arrangement in a basket near the candle.

My schnauzer, Winston, woke me by barking like crazy and finally pulling the covers off me completely. By the time I was awake enough to realize what was happening, the place was filled with smoke. I called to Trish down the hall, and we both worked to get Bill awake and out of the house just as firefighters arrived. Smoke was heavy, but we were all safe, thanks to a little dog that would not let up. He forever will be my hero.

God's mercy sees our every need and loves us so much that he sends help when we send up distress signals, or in my case, even if we don't. And his aid is not dependent on whether we think we deserve it or not. God knows that we don't deserve his love based on anything we've done. God chose to love us, save us, give us worth.

In fact, in our weakest state, God's mercy flows freely. When we are struggling the most, God knows just which life preserver to throw out.

If you are in need of mercy from God, ask him for it and trust that he will answer. If God is calling you to show mercy to someone, then forgive and love as God does—regardless of the apparent worthiness of the other person. Ask God to enlighten you to the call for mercy around you so that you can be someone's hero. And open your arms to accept all the mercy and compassion your father has for you, too!—d.o.

About the Authors

Kim McLean and Devon O'Day are hosts of FoxNews Radio's *Plain Jane Wisdom* heard nightly on www.wlac.com and on WSIX Nashville's Country Spirit Show on Sundays. They have collaborated on songs recorded by Pam Tillis, Lee Ann Womack, and many others, as well as a book/CD project purposed for pet bereavement called *Goodbye, My Friend* (Thomas Nelson Publishers). Both are on the board of Come to the Fire Women's Conferences and travel extensively in ministry with music, message, and testimony. Together, they created the Sweet Tea Tour with music and a legacy collection of recipes called *My Southern Food*.

Websites include:

www.KimMcLean.com

www.PlainJaneWisdom.com

www.PawsToReflectBook.blogspot.com

Kim McLean / Devon O'Day

P.O. Box 3

Kingston Springs, TN 37082

plainjanewisdom@gmail.com (Also on Twitter, Facebook, and LinkedIn)

CPSIA information can be obtained
at www.ICGtesting.com
Printed in the USA
LVOW01s0133010716
494813LV00008B/11/P